THE HOUSE OF THE TITANS
AND OTHER POEMS

THE HOUSE OF THE TITANS

AND OTHER POEMS

Æ

(GEORGE WILLIAM RUSSELL)

WILDSIDE PRESS

THE HOUSE OF THE TITANS AND OTHER POEMS

Originally published in 1935.

This edition published in 2008 by Wildside Press.
www.wildsidepress.com

CONTENTS

TO OSBORN BERGIN

Dear Osborn, not only because you are my friend,
But that you are one of those who learned
An ancient speech for us, who rediscovered
Myths, once the scriptures of the northern world,
I bring this poem, half dream, half vision, to you.
I know, incredulous scholar, you will lift
Ironic eyebrows as you read the tale.
But being poet yourself you will forgive
Unto the poet things unpardonable
Done by a scholar. Yet I would defend
My telling of the tale. These myths were born
Out of the spirit of man and drew their meaning
From that unplumbed profundity. I think
In after ages they will speak to us
With deeper voices and meanings. In one age
Men turn to the world about them and forget
Their old descent from heaven. In another
They storm the heavens with supplication. Some
Have found the glittering gates to open. I
Beat many times upon the gates, but was not
Like those who kept them mightily apart
Until they entered. Yet from fleeting voices
And visionary lights a meaning came
That made my myth contemporary. And those
Who read may find titans and king within
Themselves. And, if they ponder further, they may,
Not in my story, but on the shining heights
Of their own spirit, hear those lordlier voices,
The ageless shepherds of the starry flocks,
They whose majestic meditation is
The music of being; unto those who hear it
Sweeter than bells upon a darkening plain
When the dim fleeces move unto the fold.

THE HOUSE OF THE TITANS

The day was dead, and in the titans' hall
The darkness gathered like some monstrous beast
Prowling from pillar unto pillar: yet
The brazen dais and the golden throne
Made a fierce twilight flickering with stars
Far in the depths. And there the sky-born king,
Nuada, now king of earth, sat motionless,
A fading radiance round his regal brows,
The sceptre of his waning rule unused,
His heart darkened, because the god within,
Slumbering or unremembering, was mute,
And no more holy fires were litten there.
Still as the king, and pale and beautiful,
A slender shape of ivory and gold,
One white hand on the throne, beside him stood
Armid, the wise child of the healing god.
The king sat bowed: but she with solemn eyes
Questioned the gloom where vast and lumbering shades,
A titan brood, the first born of the earth,
Cried with harsh voices and made an uproar there
In the king's dun oblivious of the king.
While Armid gazed upon them came a pain
That stirred the spirit stillness of her eyes,
And darkened them with grief. Then came her words
"Tell me our story, god-descended king,
For we have dwindled down, and from ourselves
Have passed away, and have forgotten all."
And at her calling "God-descended king"
His head sank lower as if the glorious words
Had crowned his brow with a too burning flame
Or mocked him with vain praise. He answered not,
For memory to the sky-born king was but
The mocking shadow of past magnificence,
Of starry dynasties slow-fading out,
The sorrow that bound him to the lord of light
He was, ere he had sunken in red clay
His deity. The immortal phantom had not yet
Revealed to him the gentler face it wears,
The tender shadow of long vanquished pain
And brightening wisdom, unto him who nears

The Land of Promise, who, in the eve of time,
Can look upon his image at the dawn
And falter not. And as King Nuada sat
With closed eyes he saw the ancient heavens,
The thrones of awe, the rainbow shining round
The ever-living in their ageless youth,
And myriads of calm immortal eyes
That vexed him when he met the wild beast glare
And sullen gloom of the dark nation he ruled,
For whom self-exiled, irrevocably
He was outcast among the gods. And then
The words of Armid came more thronged with grief
"O, you, our star of knowledge, unto you
We look for light, to you alone.
All these Fall in that ancient anarchy again
When sorrowing you put the sceptre by.
Would not your sorrow shared melt in our love?
Or our confederate grief might grow to power,
And shake the gods or demons who decreed
This darkness for us? Or if the tale forbade
All hope, there is a sorrowful delight
In coming to the very end of all,
The pain which is the utmost life can bear,
Where dread is done, and only what we know
Must be endured, and there is peace in pain.
I would know all, O god-descended king!"
That tribe of monstrous and misshapen folk
Whose clamor overlaid her speech, and made
Its music a low murmur, had grown still
Far down the hall. And at the close her words
Came clear and purely, mingling with a voice
And harp that hushed the titans. Ah, that voice
That made the giants' ponderous bulk to faint
And bent the shaggy heads low on great hands,
While over the dark crouching figures towered
Angus the Young, the well-beloved god,
With proud tossed golden hair that glittered o'er
The beautiful bare arms that caught the harp,
And the bright form went swaying as he played.
And there were scarlet birds, a phantom throng
That dashed against the strings, and fled away
In misty flame amid the brooding crowd,
And vanished; while the colored dusk grew warm

To the imagination, and was dense
With dark heart-melting eyes, alluring lips,
With milk-white bosoms, and with glimmering arms
That drew the soul unto their folding love.
And the tormented giants groaned and lay
Prone on the hall, or stretched out hairy arms
With knotted fingers feeling for the feet
Of him who played. But the enchanter laughed,
The pride of the brute tamer in his eyes,
And looked at Armid.   She had hidden her face
To shut the vision, for he seemed no more
Before her, but a fleshless creature stalked
With bony fingers clutching at the strings,
And all the giant nation lust-consumed
Were dwindling out. "Is there no hope," she cried,
"For them, for us; or must we still forget,
And have not even memory we were gods,
And these drop to that lightless anarchy
From which they rose." Her tears were falling fast,
The gods had learned to weep, the earth's first gift.
Her weeping roused at length that stony king,
Whose face from its own shadow lifted up
Was like the white uprising of the moon.
"O" better that remembrance be no more,
Than we whose feet are tied unto this world
Should seek in phantasy to climb the thrones
Where once we sat and ruled the stars, and all
The solemn cyclic motion of these spheres.
And will the younger gods who took our seats
Call to us and descend to give us place,
Us who are feeble, who have lost our brightness,
Whom only these acknowledge; these alone
When by our arts we change their hearts' desires,
Masking their hideous shapes with airy forms,
With sheeny silver, lustrous pearl, pale gold,
Out of that glory still within us. No
'Twere better that all memory should die,"
"Let it not die," cried Armid, flinging up
In fountainous motion her white hands and arms
That wavered, then went downward, casting out
Denial. "Let it not die. Let us still be
Even in heart-torturing remembrance bound
To what we were. For that ancestral self

May wake from out this pitiful dream of ours
If there should mingle with it gleam or tone
Of its own natural majesty. I think
That unremembered world where we were born
Is not far from us, yearns for us. Sometimes
The air grows fragile and a light breaks through,
And the tall heaven leans down to touch our brows,
And our high kinsmen see us, and they are saying
Of us, 'Soon they will awaken, soon
Will come to us again.' And for a moment
We almost mix in their eternity."
Then, kneeling on the dais nigh the throne,
She cast her arms upon the high king's knees,
And took his hands, her drooping loveliness
All shaken with appeal. "Tell me, I fear
To melt into the blackness of this world,
To know naught else and yet to hate it still,
To lose the heavens yet not to be of earth,
Its natural happiness not mine. O that
Would be the blackest torture of the soul.
To forget ourselves, not to know, to hate,
To grow at last like all we hate. To have
No hope but that the darkness owns. I shall
Go mad unless you speak and tell me all."
And then the high king told her all the tale,
Which he alone remembered but in myth
And symbol. It was so very long ago
It might be but a dream, and thus it ran.
In the beginning was the boundless Lir
Within whose being heaven and earth were lost,
And Light and Dark cradled together lay,
And all things were at peace within the fold.
The hunter with the hunted lay, for each
Had found the end of battle and of hate
Was adoration. There fierce things made gentle,
And timid things made bold, and small made great,
Mingled together at the Feast of Age.
And then the long night closed. The day began
And out of the Immeasurable deep,
The habitation of eternity,
Flared the high legions of the Light and Dark.
Driving their tributary powers to build
Ethereal realms and dim underworlds.

And in the overworld from rarest fire
And starry substances, the builders reared
Murias, Gorlas, Findias and Falias,
That were like living creatures, and towered and glowed
And changed with the imagination. In those
First realms of immortal youth the gods
Had everywhere their hearts' desire. For them
Cities soared heavenward even at the thought,
And life was beautiful as it was dreamed,
For every thought broke into instant light
Around the burning multitudes of heaven.
And fluid nature, ever mirroring
The gods within Its glowing glass, was slave
To them, and held its tyranny far off.
And there the sorceress writhing in her mists
Shaped her fierce powers in hateful effigies
Of heaven and of heaven's shining hosts.
And there her children fought blind battles. There
Her stony kings held awful court. And there
The only ecstasy life knew was pain,
And torture was the only sacrifice
That could propitiate their demon gods.
Long ages inarticulate with pain
Passed by before their cry pierced up to heaven.

In that wide palace of the overworld
Where Nuada was king, the gods sat dumb
Between the lustrous pillars, on long lines
Of thrones, that faded, glow by glow, to where
The king on high sat aureoled with light.
And all were silent for that shining air
That bathed them and was both light and sound together,
And made a magic music for the gods,
The sweet notes trembling of themselves, had cried,
Not as its wont, interpreting their joy,
But as if stricken by some frenzied hand,
And the wild notes of woe went shrilling on
And chilled the shuddering gods. So all sat mute
Frozen in starlike beauty on their thrones;
For that they knew the lovely idleness
Of youth in heaven was over, and ended all
The entranced hours and foam-gay life. And now
The Realm of the Living Heart, no more

Inviolate, was stormed by sorrow, and they,
Who feared no strife with elemental powers,
Being themselves the masters of the fire,
Must war with sorrow, a spirit thing, that feared
No battlement that cast forth lightnings, but
Came cowled invisibly past watch and ward,
And none knew till it keened within the heart.
When Nuada within the darkling hall
Saw all the bowed heads of his sovereignty,
The stricken children of the mighty Lir,
He heard a voice within him crying, "Sorrow
Has come upon you. Rise and war on sorrow."
And to his eyes the underworld cast up
Its nameless horrors 'mid the hall of heaven,
Dim tyrannies that aped the sway of light,
And grotesque idols of enormous bulk
Carved by some gnomic art that never felt
The spirit thrill of beauty. And he saw
The altars smoking with the victim's blood,
Where lips were dumb through hopelessness, but yet
From the most inner living heart of these
A cry went to the heart of all the world,
And made that wild distracted melody
That shook the gods. Then Nuada arose,
A blazing torch of indignation, and called,
And in his voice rang out such pity and wrath,
The proud and golden races flashed and leaped
Dilated unimaginably for war,
With dragon crests of ruby and of gold
That flamed o'er burning faces and lit eyes,
Till all the hall was dense with forms of fire,
The warrior magnificence of heaven,
That, in a many-colored torrent, streamed
From shining courts and from the lawns of light
And swayed there to and fro with brandished fires
Clenched in uplifted hands. They shouted loud
Responding to the call of the high king.
And Nuada spake thus unto the host.
"This is the ending of the golden age,
For that we know from ancient prophecy
That darkness more intense than light has grown
To shake the strings that for the mightiest
Alone have voice. And we must hear them breathe

Their melody of anguish age by age
Until the very heavens are wrecked of joy,
And we be crushed, as in that tyranny
Where our dark brother Balor rules the gloom,
Save we can overcome that tyranny.
Though we be children of the mighty Lir,
And though his might be in us to create,
Yet what is built is only what we dream,
And so it comes these heavens alone are holy
Because of things that we imagine there.
If, by the magic of the mighty Lir,
Cities spring heavenward even at our thought
And life is beautiful but as we dream,
Our grief too shall discolor paradise
And dim these glittering cities. Ye have heard
The Children of the Darkness cry to us.
And we who are the Children of the Light
Must answer in the infinite brotherhood.
Who will go with me to that underworld
Where Balor for an iron age hath made
Anguish immutable? Who ventures there
Must wear the very body of death, and feel
The very soul of hate gnaw in his heart;
And can but overcome them so he use
The tender and fierce fire of spirit alone."
Out of his wider vision spake the king
Of that abysmal life that underlay
The Happy Plains. But they of heaven heard
The tale unfearing. When the high king called,
"Who will go with me, warriors of heaven?"
A foam of glorious faces swayed to him
Athirst for the heroic enterprise.
And then the mightiest, rising from their thrones,
Offered each one his own peculiar powers.
"To earth I give the magic of the mind,"
Said Manannan, nighest of all to Lir.
And Dana said, "I shall make beauty there."
And Angus said, "My birds shall waken love."
Ogma, "The might of heaven is Mine to give."
Fintan, "I shall bring memory and hope."
"And I shall be the vanishing of pain,"
Said Diancecht. And of the immortals none
But would lay down his sceptre, and forgo

The sweetness of his youth on such a quest.
After long pondering and council sought
Where the All-Father breathed his oracles,
Forth fared the heavenly adventurers,
The chosen of Lir's children, passing from
The old, perpetual, rejoicing life,
Where in the lucid being of the gods
The Mighty Father, shining, made each one
A mirror of his own infinitudes.
Then weaving forms of magic power that might
Withstand the elemental energies,
Upon the mid world venturing, the gods
Down the sidereal streams waned far away
From the ancestral plains and Light of Lights.
And lastly by aeonian journeyings
Came unto earth, the desert verge of things,
Where all the heavens once held within their hearts
Were now without, beyond, and far away.
And as a spider by the finest thread
Hangs from the rafters, so the sky-born hung
By but the frailest thread of memory from
The habitations of eternity.
Yet still about them clung a heavenly air,
The shadow of their ancient nobleness;
And gods they seemed unto the titan brood,
Sovereign hitherto on earth. And these,
All wonderstruck before the heaven-born,
Were prostrate, and thereafter made them kings,
Served them and worked their will, and built for them
Cyclopean duns, massy, of bronze or stone
The time defying and unchangeable
Fabric of earth. And so, because the gods
Were folk of many arts, and all had drunk
The Well of Knowledge, every work they planned
Was marvelous unto the earth-born tribes
Suppliant of all that wisdom. For a time
The heavenly quest seemed won, the face of earth
Turned to the skies. But underneath it all
Some evil sorcery worked on the gods,
And from them one by one dropped memory,
So that it came they knew no light but that
Set in the sky, the bodily form to be
Themselves. And earth had lost its first

Impenetrable strangeness and grew dear
As hearth and home. And they had happiness
Moving amid its woods, rivers and hills.
Only sometimes when gazing on the night,
Freckled with myriad fires, they sighed and knew
Not why they sighed. Or when the flaming sun
Sank drowned in darkness it seemed a secret tale
Was told of their own falling. They thought no more
Of that transfiguration of titan into god
They had imagined; and half a fable it seemed
That story of heroic enterprise,
And then it was forgotten utterly.
The children of earth grew noble to their eyes,
And they took brides from them, and through the gods
The titan brood inherited the fires,
Lights that made starry dreams of pride or power.
And last the being of the gods was changed
To be but lordlier titan, and their king
Seemed but a madman dreaming of lost worlds.
Then when the tale was told, with desperate eyes
Armid gazed into the cyclopean dark,
And to her imagination or spirit sense
The brazen gloom was quick with livid shapes,
Monstrosities of soul that in themselves
Downward and backward prowl unto the brute.
And here a ghoul, ice green, with famished eyes
Glared at her where a titan's head had been;
There apes that gibbered obscenely, monstrous cats
That bristled with cold lights, and snaky heads,
And dark implacable eyes of birds of prey
That burned like evil fires within the gloom.
But yet more terrible unto her heart
The conflagration heaven had made on earth
Breathing ethereal fire into red clay,
Revealing beauty invisible before,
The fairy star that glimmered o'er white brows,
The lights that danced upon the airy limbs,
The bloom and shadow as of delicate flowers
That flickered over the sweet breasts, and dazzled
The titans with strange graces. And, because
The body cannot clasp the phantom glow,
The soul wrought wantonness and unnameable
Defilement upon spirit. Armid saw

The beauty of the sky-maidens violated
By the passionate imagination, and she reeled
Sick with the horror, stretching out blind hands,
For it was Angus by his song had kindled
Desire so high that the sky maidens only
Could satisfy the god-created lust.
Then she groped outward for the mighty gates,
And stood there trembling like a moth. The night,
Black framed between the pillar posts of bronze,
Glowed like a fiery furnace of blue flame,
With heavens that lost themselves in their own depths,
Rumoring their own infinitudes,
Fainting and faltering in their speech, for light,
Though swiftest of all things, ere it has found
A resting Place or hamlet in the gloom
The worlds it spake of have long ceased to be.
As inaccessible as those dim lights
The heavens from which the gods had fallen so far,
From infinite to pigmy. Armid beat
Upon her breast at her own impotence.
Then the pure daughter of Diancecht
Felt a fierce heat invade her, and she saw
A titan with his red and bestial eyes
Fixed on her beauty. The divine maid shuddered
Through all her virgin being in premonition
Of martyrdom through long ages to be,
Of beauty bowed to sorrow, overborne
By the unleashed brute in the titan heart.
And the divine maid, maddened by her fears,
Raced the dark lawn and onward to the beach,
When the cold waters stayed her, and she paused,
Holding her heart that fluttered like a bird
At the long peril of the night in time.
And then at last she sat upon a stone
Gazing into the night, and heard the roar
Of undistinguishable waters, until
Upon the far horizon glowed a star,
A star that rose where the late sun had set,
A light dilating that came swiftly to her,
And there were flutterings within the light
As of celestial plumes fanning the air.
And in the brightness there were fiery creatures,
A winged horse, and o'er the rider's brow

A sunrise blazed. The winged courser came,
Trampling the glittering billows, and before it
The light flared on, revealing the wild surges,
That had been before invisible, leaping up
In shadowy shining, and, like hurrying clouds,
Beaten by the storm of light unto the shore,
Where the thick smoke of foam rolled on the sands
And broke, frothing with stars. Armid arose
Her head bowed unto the glory of light,
And when she lifted it the winged creature
Had flown, but a tall warrior, its rider,
Stood by her, a pillar of flame, his eyes so still
They might have watched only eternities.
She heard a voice that seemed soundless, that spoke
To the spirit ear. "Tell the high king a champion
Out of the Land of Promise comes to him."
And with no word the daughter of Diancecht
As one in trance, not moved by her own will,
Walked to the great gateway. Unterrified
She passed that titan who had frighted her,
And came to the high king and told her tale.
But he, obscured within himself, said only
"What mightier warrior was there in heaven
Than Ogma. Now he leads the giants in war.
Tell thou that champion to fly his winged horse,
Swift as its frantic plumes may carry, before
The sorcery overcome him and he forgets."
Then Armid came again to him who stood,
A stillness in flame, unseen by any eye
But hers, and spoke as the high king had said.
That voice again spoke to her spirit ear.
"I am an enchanter. Say this to the high king."
So Armid spake to Nuada, but he:
"Who had more enchantments than Dana, who made
The primal forms of beauty for the gods.
Now upon brute imaginings she casts
Her glamour. What need have we for enchanters!
So to the heavenly wizard Armid brought
The king's denial: and he to her said,
"Go To the high king, and say a poet waits
Upon his threshold." And at this the king
Spoke more disdainfully. "Have we not Angus,
The poet whose song could recreate in us

The ancientness before the worlds, where we,
Lost in each other's being, found a honey
Hoarded for us we could not find in time,
A song we hear no more. For now that poet
Praises beauty that is but redness of clay.
And the mad winging of his fiery birds
Kindles the torment of infinite desire
For shapes so fleeting they are hardly born
Ere they are crumbled. Say unto that poet
There are too dark shadows about us for song."
Once more came Armid, as one in trance, unto
That heavenly poet forbidden song, who said,
"I know the story of things past. I know
The tale of things to be." And to the king
She came as bidden by the master of time
And spoke. But the king said, "Was not Fintan
Historian and prophet! Now his history runs
Backward to the abyss. His prophecies
Tell only of worlds lightless and frozen, where we
Shall have for cairn the glaciers over us.
We need no prophet." And the maiden told
Unto that seer what the high king had said.
And he who came from out a timeless world
Spoke to her. "I am a healer." And once more
She stood before the throne. But Nuada cried,
"A healer too! Have we not Diancecht!
What need have we for another god to tend
The blighted in mind or body, who are leprous
With evil living, so that desire may be
Fierce as before. That is no labor for gods."
And then, forbidden healing, that lordly one
Spake unto Armid, "Go thou to the high king
And say I am a shepherd. I have wisdom
To guide the starry flocks." And on swift feet
As if that shepherd of stars had guided her,
She passed the reeling titans and stood before
The throne, and spoke even as the shepherd said.
But Nuada answered. "Had not the Son of Lir
All wisdom! Through him those who had only
Blind strength have grown crafty to conspire
Even against the gods. Say to that one
It is easier to rule the heavens than the earth."
And at this last denial the wise one said,

"Ask the high king has he in that dark house
One who is master of so many arts."
And at this saying the high king sat upright
As if a star had lighted the abyss
Of memory, and it had recreated
An ancient glory. And he cried to Armid,
"Bring unto me that master of many arts."
And Armid went more swiftly, wondering
If he who had been so many times denied
Still waited. In her imagination of him
He was not single but innumerable,
And all the stars and heavens were dancing in
Her thoughts that bowed before him. But when she
Passed through the gateway into the night that one
Who would not be denied still waited there.
Once more she looked into the ageless eyes,
And spoke the high king's words, and led the way
Through the great gateway to the brazen gloom.
While Nuada was sunken in himself
A clamor of giant voices filled the hall,
The fierce titans disputing, and the darkness
Shook as at night the mountain valleys shake
When dragon and mad colossi roar from their caves.
And the king woke and cried out terribly
Smiting the echoing gong. "It is not fitting
For slaves to brawl in presence of their king."
And at his words the titans crouching were mute.
For when the high king willed they must obey,
His will burning like fire, and it had power
To slay or to create. Then Armid came
And with her came the master of many arts.
And it may be because she had spoken with gods
And was raised above herself, to the sky maiden
The titans, so fearful before, now seemed remote
As the far stars had been to her sadness. None
But the high king and Armid saw the god.
The daughter of Diancecht then sat apart
With bowed head in the shadow of the throne,
And heard voices above her of great beings,
And saw a circle of the shining ones
In the dark radiance under shuttered eyes.
She heard first the voice of the high king
Who spoke as one who was awaking from sleep

Unto the heavenly visitor, "Why hast thou,
Riding the horse of dawn, come to this place,
To us forgotten in heaven. For it must
Be but a legend of its dawn, the story
Of those rebel against its joy, who thought
To overcome the anarchs of the abyss
And were themselves overcome. If thou
Hast from pity come to help us, fly.
There were immortals shining as thou art,
And now they know not who they are, or from
What heaven they fell. It may be that I too
Shall grow like these who have forgotten all,
Be darkened, nor know of any other world."
And he who came from the ancestral light
Said, "Thou are indeed darkened to dream
Of these that any had been gods. Thou only
Art real, these, but shadows of immortals.
Since thou art darkened I will enter thee
Giving my light to see the unfallen lights.
Thou shalt hear voices speaking from thy own depths,
And know to what evocation they will answer
And dwell with thee even in this dark house."
And while he spoke the thick and evil gloom
Was paling within the titans' hall, and earth
Grew shadowy thin, then dropped away. A light
Dawned through the darkness like a fiery sun
Risen within the world. The crouching titans
Gave place unto a lordlier company
Of the star-crested Ever-Living Ones,
With eyes of ageless ecstasy, and faces
Holy, compassionate, inexorable,
With voices speaking the law of their high being
Unto the king. And, in an air that was
Both music and light together, the poet of heaven,
A brightness within the light, came singing to him
As if his song rose from the sun of life.
"O, see our sun is dawning for us, ever dawning
With ever youthful and exulting voices.
Your sun is but a smoky shadow: ours
The ruddy and eternal glow. Your fire
Is far away, but ours within our hearts
Is ever living, and through wood and wave
Is ever dawning on adoring eyes.

Do you not know me? I am the All-Father's voice.
Until die twilight of the ages comes
I sing the deathless union between all things.
My birds from crystal-fiery plumage shed
The Light of Lights. Their kisses wake the love
That never dies and leads through death to me.
I am in every love. But when they cling
Unto the hands, the lips, the eyes, my song
Is silent. I fly and vanish and return not
Till the red flutterings of the heart are still.
I live in every love, but it is lightless
Until they know the love they seek through me
Is not the single but the innumerable joy:
Until desire has made them pass away
From their own selves for ever, and they cry
To the All-Father to give to them his death,
The dark rapture where they are lost in him.
I am known only to self forgetfulness.
My love shall be in thine when love is sacrifice."
And then most pitying, most inexorable,
As from a shoreless sea of wisdom came
The voice of unappeasable law, so still
It seemed to waver between life and death.
"Do not turn from me. Think on me long and long.
Though I am justice and implacable,
And nothing can escape me, no least erring,
Yet am I also mercy and forgiveness.
The pain I give is healing and guidance. It draws
The marred in body and mind, the lost and strayed
Back unto life, and to the path that leads
Unto their high inevitable destiny
Of beauty and delight. In those who mourn
Their well-beloved dead I am the secret
Sweetness they find in sorrow, coming to know
That all was heavenly guided. And that wisdom
Is absolution for their sins, and they
Join in the cavalcade of starry minds.
Know that all wisdom bides in joy or pain.
When the mysterious river runs in channels
Made clear by the pure spirit, its name is joy.
But when the soul is thickened and dark the stream
Breaks through and tends till all is purified
By the sweet water. Those who know me thus

Find joy in pain. They even press the spear
For swifter absolution into the heart.
I shall be with thee when thy will, no more
Rebel, shall know that I am justice, and cry
'Hail unto thee! and hail! and hail for ever!'
Although I come to thee as death, or strike
At love that is more even to thee than life.
Yield to me and thou art my conqueror.
There is no other god than me to fear."
So spake the ancestral voice of Diancecht,
And after that dread wisdom came the voice
Of Dana, mother of all and comforter.
"I am the tender voice calling away,
Whispering between the beatings of the heart,
And inaccessible in dewy eyes
I dwell, and all unkissed on lovely lips,
Lingering between white breasts inviolate,
And fleeting ever from the passionate touch,
I shine afar till men may not divine
Whether it is the stars or the beloved
They follow with rapt spirit. And I weave
My spells at evening, folding with dim caress,
Aerial arms and twilight dropping hair,
The lonely wanderer by wood or shore,
Till, filled with some vast tenderness, he yields,
Feeling in dreams for the dear mother heart
He knew ere he forsook the starry way,
And clings there pillowed far above the smoke
And the dim murmur from the duns of men.
I can enchant the rocks and trees, and fill
The dumb brown lips of earth with mystery,
Make them reveal or hide the god; myself
Mother of all, but without hands to heal,
Too vast and vague, they know me not, but yet
I am the heartbreak over fallen things,
The sudden gentleness that stays the blow,
And I am in the kiss that foemen give
Pausing in battle, and in the tears that fall
Over the vanquished foe. And in the highest
Among the Danann gods I am the last
Council of pity in their hearts when they
Mete Justice from a thousand starry thrones.
My heart shall be in thine when thine forgives."

After the voice of ancient beauty had died
The voice of Ogma, the master of the fires:
"Though I have might to roll the stars through heaven,
And all the gods are suppliant of my power,
And what they do is portion of my strength,
I was made master by the All-Father only
Because I was the gentlest of the gods.
And, though I make fierce war upon the anarchs,
My myrmidons are frail and delicate things.
I hide within a blossom and its still beauty
Becomes mighty as a star and none may touch it.
I can stay the march of armies by a child.
When I look through its eyes the passionate hand
Falls, and the soul in awful penitence
Hides in itself. And with a twilight air
I can make anchorites of kings. I overcome
Fierce things by gentleness. And my allies
Against the thunder of congregated powers
Are silences in heaven, the light in valleys,
The smoke above the roof, the quiet hearth,
The well-beloved things that come to be
Images of peace in the All-Father's being.
No sentinel can stay them, and they make
Traitors to glory and pride. And so I gather
Invincible armies that can invade
The secret places of the spirit, until
Even the comets and mad meteors,
The lions of the wilderness of space,
Who roam with fiery manes, the potentates
Of air and earth, rulers of thrones and powers,
Melted within themselves give fealty,
And build together till the dream of life
Mirrors the All-Father's being, and that
Can know itself in us as we in him.
When thou art of thine own will defenceless
As the fragile flickering moth or trembling grass,
I shall be champion for thee. Thou shalt find
Invisible legions breathing love for thee
Through the dark clay, or from the murmuring air,
And by the margin of the deep. And when
Thy spirit becomes so gentle it could pass
Into another spirit and leave no wound,
I will give unto thee this star to lead."

Then came the voice of Fintan, the master of time.
"I am all knowledge, all that was or is
Or ever shall be glows and breathes in me
In an eternal present. Even the gods
Departing from me are lost within themselves,
And slave to the enchantment that divides
Has-been from yet-to-come and far from near.
So they forget themselves and dwindle down
From their full orbit. And they come to be
Frail sparks that wander in the immensity
Of their own primal being, moving ever
Unto horizons that forever recede.
Yet am I always with them. I abide
Steadfast, the still innumerable light,
Between the vanished and the coming wave.
And yet they know me not. Incessant voices
In every beating of the heart will call
Away from me. For one will cry to them,
'O hurry, hurry to the golden age.'
And yet another voice appeals,
'O come. A treasure lies in the rich wilderness.
There is the fountain of youth.' Others will cry:
'Go not.' 'Thy love is dying.' 'Thy friend is false.
'Thine enemy derides thee.' 'That tyrant crush.'
'Let us be conqueror,' or 'All is lost!'
Though they fly from me it is me they seek,
Nor know that I am in their every breath.
When unto these loud voices thy heart is blind,
And hope and fear are dead, and thou art still
Amid the battle thunder, and desire not
Sceptre nor crown. Then I shall be with thee
And melt for thee the heavens into one light,
And shepherd the long aeons into one fold
With all dead beauty and beauty yet unborn,
And enemies made lovers, and dread monsters
Become gentle and spirit things. Desiring nothing
I will give thee all." And last of these
Immortal voices spake the Son of Lir.
"I am the shepherd of the starry flocks,
The wisdom of the gods. And it is mine
To plan for every spirit, even the worm
And tiny gnat, their path through winding cycles
Until they glow with uncreated light

And blaze with power. And those who sat on thrones
And shone like gods at dawn of the great day
I bring to the abyss where they are dimmed,
But not for their abasing. Those who know
The heavens only are but slaves of light,
Mirrors of majesties they are not, shining
In beauty given to them, not their own,
Nor born from their own valor. For to be
True gods, self-moving, they must grow to power
Warring in chaos with anarchs. It was I
Who broke thy trance upon the Happy Plains
Revealing to thee the underworld. And yet
It was thy will made thee heroical
And rebel to that joy. All the high gods
Have made the sacrifice of heaven, and worn
Dark clay around their light; and in the abyss
Have known unnumbered sorrows, and the joy
Of every creature, and come to myriad wisdom,
A honey harvested from many lives.
And so the primal vision is for them
Transfigured into being. For thy first
Heroical will to conquer thou must conceive
Thyself as spirit to all nature, and
All life that breathes within it to be thy own.
When thou canst beat upon its myriad gates
Crying, 'It is thyself that comes,' all gates
Will open for thee; and the love that dwells
In hate will burst its dungeon, and fly to thee
As children fly to a beloved breast.
High majesties shall be melted unto thee,
The dragons of the waste be gentle, and
The slave with thee be fearless and a king
In his own heart, and the dumb mind have voice,
And every spirit reveal the wonder concealed
In its own depths. And when thou knowest all
Thou shalt be counselor with the high gods
Who pass remembering through the nights and days
Of the All-Father, and at the Feast of Age
Be with them when they plan for the new dawn
Glories beyond all ever known. When thou
Shalt pray, not for thyself, but for those others
I will give thee the wisdom of eternity."
The master of many arts was heard no more.

The heaven-descended voices died in deeps
Of the king's being. The starry shining shapes
Through which the lords had utterance vanished. But
Before the tide of darkness had returned,
And by their mingled light of vision, he saw
Within the titan heart, and felt its beating
As he were one with it; and all the wonder
And awe at the sky visitors; the beauty
Unimaginable on earth before;
And last, desire to hold, to own, to be:
The tumult of unappeasable desire
For loveliness that is of spirit alone
Eluding the titan arm, leaving to it
Only the primal clay; the titan trust
In strength, the error oft repeated, and
The brute despair and the descent to hells
Earth had not known before the spirit came.
Until from pain and fiery penitence
And brooding, and self pity that came to be
All pitiful, slowly die titan heart
Found in its depths the magian mind that can
Grow what it dreams on. And through its worship came
Transfigurations, and the adoring heart
Passed from itself; its ancient sorrows grown
To be its blessings, its agonies become
Its joys, the titan darkness to blaze with stars,
And the high powers that only yield themselves
To gentleness, awaiting its perfecting to give
Sovereignty over all the elements.
As one who reaps the harvest of ages at once
He saw the titan thought invade the world,
Run through its veins, until the silence broke
With revelation; and the earth became
A mother speaking to her children, giving
The wisdom of her heavenly ways; her dawns,
Her noons, her twilights magical with love;
Life breathing life, no longer solitary.
Its every breathing quick with multitude:
The infinite above them with its lights
From its majestical remoteness bent
With voices and meanings from the vast, and earth
Casting its robe of darkness to reassume
Its ancient garment of light; and in divine

Companionship waiting the tremor that runs
Throughout the Spheres when the All-Father calls
His children homeward; and the high grandees,
The very noblest in the universe,
Princes of stars, and solar kings, and rulers
Of constellations and of galaxies,
Are bowed in awe, and put aside their sceptres,
As humble as the least of creeping things
Before the mystery of the All-Father,
The illimitable, whom none had ever known
Though lost within him at the Feast of Age,
So the high king, rapt in his vision, dreamed
Of that great hostel at the end of time
Where all the cycles sleep; and came at last
To open his eyes upon the brazen gloom
To know the labor before him, and to hear
The titans raving madly in the hall.

LOST TALISMAN

Those images of beauty
That once I did despise,
Now in my age I cherish
And clutch with miser's eyes.
Even for one frail blossom
I will make sacrifice.

Once there were other treasures
I had, O strange to say,
Made dim those magic blossoms
And I cast them away.
I cast beauty from me
As a god child might in play.

O what was in the being
Of boyhood that could make
Beauty seem but a glimmer
That followed in the wake
Of some proud sails set sunward
On some enchanted lake.

COMFORT

The skies were dim and vast and deep
Above the vale of rest.
They seemed to rock the stars to sleep
Beyond the mountain's crest.

I sought for graves I had mourned, but found
The roads were blind. The grave,
Even of love, heart-lost, was drowned
Under time's brimming wave.

Huddled beneath the wheeling sky,
Strange was my comfort there:
That stars and stones and love and I
Drew to one sepulchre.

A MOUNTAIN TARN

The pool glowed to a magic cauldron
O'er which I bent alone.
The sun burned fiercely on the waters,
The setting sun:
A madness of fire: around it
A dark glory of stone.

O mystic fire!
Stillness of earth and air!
That burning silence I
For an instant share.
In the crystal of quiet I gaze
And the god is there.

Within that loneliness
What multitude!
In the silence what ancient promise
Again renewed!
Then the wonder goes from the stones,
The lake and the shadowy wood.

WOOD WAYS

Thus did the laughing king, the magic maker,
Draw me into the wind-glittering wood
By an enchantment of blown boughs and lights,
And faint and myriad flickerings within
The many-pillared palace of leaves. The air,
A flying girl, flame-limbed, before me runs
Sprinkling the dark with jewels. Eyes are dizzy
With sudden color. O, the hyacinths!
I fall on knees watching the laughing king
Hide stars in wild blossoms. On moss I lie,
My eyes are shuttered but the earth is airy,
Dense to the body, to the spirit most clear.
O, it was so in the golden age. Men lived
In the bright fire, in air, in earth. They knew
Only the being of the laughing king
And had no name for themselves. A night
Of many million years breaks now to dawn.
As the numbed limb quickening to life becomes
Once more the body we knew, so the whole star
Quickens within me. Why was the spirit numb
In a little dust? I glow to the full orb.
Upon its burnished uplands what shining dancers,
With what unfallen beauty, what wild innocence
Make visible the laughter of their king!
By what fleet witchery of limb the inaudible
Becomes music to the eye, joy in the heart!
What secret lies behind the lovely light?
What lovelier darkness, from which spirit-clear
Voices call to me, "O, come home, come home!"

DISTRACTION

I lapsr from her sweet play.
   Although My heart had hardly beat
For a dream instant, the wild child
   Stamps with imperious feet.

Wind-quickened shook the forest boughs;
   Green. glitterings died and came;
O'er her young stormy beauty broke
   Ripples of shade and flame.

I wake, my lovely child, I wake;
   I fly thy slave to be.
Forgive, O voices from the deep,
   Yet come again to me.

TIME SPIRITS

I Do not chide them that they fly the wood,
Hill, river, lake, remote and endless shore,
Nor pluck jewels of words out of the light,
But seek their song under those cliffs of stone
And stone-gray air that reels dizzy with mist.
They think if they but watch their world they will
Be master of it, their speech recall today
Unto tomorrow. They do not know that time
Forgets its hours, its days, its years and all
But that which has some touch of the timeless on it.
We do not care to know of Plato's town
By what light arts, what trick of life, men made
The color of their days. But we remember
One who by airy labors found a way
From earth to heaven, and looked upon a sea,
Shoreless, of beauty, and told of it in words
Dipt in its shining. I have no blame that they
Forget the aristocracy of speech, and use
Slang of the town, and have no age in their thought,
And think as children might do if their world
Were newly born, and god or sage had never
Dropt star or lantern into our abyss:
Or look on frailty, seeing the skimming dancers
With lightness of feet lighten the leaden heart,
Jetting gay fire into the fireless mind.
They might look upon transience all day long
Yet be in company of the gods, could they
But know the Master of the Ceremony,
Cry with Aratus, "Full of Zeus the city:
Full of Zeus the harbor; and full of Zeus
Are all the ways of men," the vision that makes
All lights be torches in the mystery,
All speech be part of the soliloquy,
Or endless canticle, all holy, sung
By Him who is poet both of heaven and earth.

TWO MAGICS

Have they the same enchantment, these children straying
In streets where electric moonlight and scintillating rose
Shed blooms on the ashen air, as those other children
Crouched in trance under hedgerows where hawthorn thickens
      its snows;

Or those others, who under a real moon and stars
Move to deeper wonder in themselves, who are still,
Who touch each other but gently, lest they break the magic
That makes them one with it on the night-shadowy hill.

DEFEAT

How easily defeated! A fleet grace of limb
Swept by; dark eyes that dared him follow where they led:
And all the heavens had dwindled to one star for him,
And the great deep lay hollow, lightless, blind and dead.

Sadly the over-shadowing forms of might depart.
His eyes with longing no more search the mystic sea.
With one alone he lingers murmuring heart to heart,
"One infinite, thy love, is life enough for me."

THE DARK LADY

O, no, I was not wanton with that man.
But to his imaginations, yes. I made
Myself a hundred natures. It is writ,
My myriad girlhood, in that printed page.
Or was it I? Did I but play the part
His magic plotted for me? Did he know
That his imaginations lived in me
And swayed me to be one of their own kind,
To act the bawd for whom an emperor
Might cast his world away: or it might be
A maid to whom the world had never come,
All innocent upon a fairy isle.
Yet at the court of the great queen I had
But one disdainful face, however many
Wild hearts might beat within me: and high lords
And admirals, who had wrecked Armadas, were
Wrecked on a flinty look. O, I remember.
My heart swoons to think upon that hour,
When a young learned gentleman, his head
Dizzy with gaudy words that had caught fire
From sun and moon, importuned me to know
The latest prince of speech. And I was swept,
Half laughing and half scornful, to my fate.
Yet I had not been one hour in the room
Ere I was lit by many torches, and
Knew, being in that humble lodging house,
That I had come unto a lordlier court
Than the great queen's, a court where kings and princes
Robeless could awe by their own majesty,
Or, being bare to the spirit, seemed as low
As if they had not legions at their call.
And there were elves that frolicked in his thought,
And giddy knaves whose very sins seemed rooted
In a wild nature, and might win them heaven
To make laughter for angels. I knew a man
Who held these very knaves had much to teach us
As the apostles: and we would lose less
Missing the queen of the dawn out of the myths,
Juno, with grave eyes under heavenly brows
And proud, starred peacocks, than if his rascal

Jack Had never lived in story. Not at once
Did I know all. No man will ever know
The mystery of his being, of multitudes
Within one spirit. Yet I knew from the first
That they were with him, incorporeal real,
Taking immortal bodies from sweet sounds,
Leaping into our thought as gay moon,
A slippery dancer, reels from wave to wave.
He had hardly spoken ere a spirit of his
Had flashed within me, and I had made answer
Out of its nature. He turned upon me eyes
So wonder-wise, so humorous kind, that I
Was melted from my art of dignity
And became once more the laughing girl who ran
Under her father's elms, who knew no rank
But life; jesting with folly; with her wit
Pelting both lords and grooms. O, the sweet play,
When all the delicate spirit's aflame, and points
With its own fire the airy rapier, nor knows
In that obscurity of delight the end
That it desires, the point in the other's breast.
For we are both half fearing and half faining
The exquisite anguish of our pierc'ed heart.
So flashed our speech. The first of many times.
I had not more easily as a small child
Told my heart stories than I could to him
Tell everything in thought, as if he were
An ampler, wiser heart-nurse to myself.
And though I was all love I shrank from that,
The mating of lips and body, lest having all
I should have less than love; in the king's bed
Be absent from his court. And when I was
Within myself, the angels of wisdom and love
Held passionate council in me. I was rent
By images of love and by their martyrdoms,
For I had buried many an image deep
In the heart's doubt what would be noble to do.
And for there was that warfare in me the girl
Was ripened to full woman. I looked back
Upon the woman I had been before
As she upon her childhood. I was I think
The only creature that by flesh and blood
Entered the court of his spirit: and all others

Came through some crystal mystic gate unto
The throne of his heart as vassals might, and left
Not tribute of pearl, ivory or gold
But breathed their very spirits into him
That he would dress as emperors and clowns,
Play one against another. I do believe
The mighty dead from unimagined homes
Dreamed back their greatness and their frailty,
The very lion front that awed the world,
Shaking it by the thunder of words that fell
From the imperious heaven of the high will.
And how could it be other? We are not gods
To create life, and only what is given us
Order and rule. I know it, I, that was
A glowing mirror to him, would sometimes,
Ere he had spoken, find living in myself
His latest imagination, the very trick
Of its mad mood, and hear it afterwards
Dressed in the actor's body cry on a stage.
If it was so with me, might he not be
A hostel for all life? For some design,
I know not what. Perhaps that we who play
Upon our surfaces might pry more deep
In our rich mystery, the way be pointed
That life must travel. I thought it so, that he
Was magicked by the gods for their design,
And I was handmaid to it. O how frail
The instruments the gods must use in us!
There came to the queen's court their masterpiece,
A boy that stayed the breath, all glow and fire,
Unflawed, so airy ivory of limb
He might have leaped from an archangel's dream.
And was it destiny that two such wonders
Of soul and body should meet, be to each other
Mystery and enchantment: beauty that had
No soul but beauty itself: and the wise soul,
Baffled in reading where there was not mind,
Fell into dreaming, and at last was stayed
On the body's miracle. And I grew sick
Seeing the dawn of an unnatural love,
The kind that marred the Grecian genius, and closed
The nobleness of mind that had begun
With Homer's tale. I cried upon myself

As all corrupt to so misread the eyes
That rested on the boy, or the sweet words.
But when I knew that I had not misread,
O, what heart shaking, what deep fountains of scorn
Or pity broke out like madness. I lay awake
Buffeted by fierce winds from heaven and hell,
Searching the blackness of my night for God.
And knew not whether God or devil counseled,
Self love, or love that crucifies itself,
Or anguish of long stemmed desire to have
What passes from it. But I thought to stay
That love unnatural test his spirit's walls
Should thicken, and there be a solitude
In that high court. And I used every art
Of heart and body and gave the body to him,
And had no joy in giving. The holy fires
Whereof the Elohim compounded us
If they glow not to one pure breathing, but
Are all disordered, war in us and burn us
By hurt of beauty or love, or wisdom cries,
A mourner in the thick of erring delight.
And he to whom I was no mystery,
But a dear friend, stayed not his heart on me,
For that infinitude of his wide mind,
Searching ever for the undiscovered heart,
Wandered away from me unto that one
Beautiful, baleful and uncharted star
Of boyhood. I knew my sacrifice was vain
And a new madness shook me, making me
All pitiless, with a mad woman's will
To win her way even if soul be lost.
And all affections in me made bitter, changed
In dark reverse unto their opposites.
I was as one who hears an angel sing
To a sweet lute, then turns to her dark angel
To sing the same song to the trembling strings,
And pure and holy are made poisonous.
When we are maddened, and the goblins in us
Riot in incredible loves and hates
I do not know if god or demon guides
The storm while we are blinded. I was not
The same although I moved to the same end.
For now I was all hopeless in love, yet played

With all my woman's art upon the boy,
Meeting him in palace chambers or
In garden alleys. I was I know not what
Unconquered and rich wonder to his youth
That had won all easily before, but now
Met but a lovely mockery when he prayed;
And the unravished beauty was to him,
As with that other, the sole star of the heart.
And so I drew him, half forgetting at times
My purpose, for he was a masterpiece
Of heaven, and how sweet to play with, till
My purpose and some wildness in my blood
Conspired together. I yielded to him, became
A mistress unto two, one godlike in mind
And one, the outer image of a god.
And in intoxication of conquest the boy
Wore all a victor's airs with me until
Even rumor had no further secrets to tell.
And then at last one day I met the other
And he had known, and never was there face
So ravaged, and my heart in every beat
Let rain a drop all fiery red. There was
I know not what wild pity in my eyes,
And the god knows that at no other time
Was I so lost from myself, so terribly his.
Yet at his anguished words I wore the air
Of one bred in the gay court of the world
Above the ceremony by which the herd
Order their ways, one who took carelessly
This love or that, and knew no obligation
But to win fuel to keep high one's fire.
He could not read me, my heart-aching humor -
For I was not then in his heart that never
Misread, but only an apparition to his eyes -
When I likened myself to him, the myriad minded
Who gathered knaves and heroes with like love
To snatch the inmost secret of them, so I
Seeking as rich a wisdom, must, being woman,
Who win only by the body, search the soul
At its full tide in the completeness of love,
When, to the vigilant spirit, it is quick
With all it is. And I had not yet won
Spirits enough to be a mate for him

Learned in so many hearts. He threw at me
A single word. I, who had masked my soul
As the proud queen of harlots to deceive,
Was yet angered he should be credulous,
And all that was still virginal in me,
And all my passion he should be deceived,
Cried furiously in bitter and wild speech
That spurned him. When god and devil through one voice
Cry the same words they scorch with double fire.
And he, the mighty seer, looked for a moment
Upon me as if spirit and sense in him
Were sundered. With no other word he went.
He saw me never again. Yet I was victor
Slaying the unnatural with the natural love.
And I do think for all my bruised heart
I was more happy than he. I can but guess
From that he made the bitter Troilus speak
Of Cressid in how many blazing fires
His anger burned me. Still I dreamed of that
Rich court so many colored once. But now,
O, what dark travelers scourged to that dark house
Brought as unto the nether sovereignty
Tribute of raving madness, guilt and fear,
Unto that one whose fearful artistry
With pigments of midnight, eclipse and fire
Could make them visible for ever.
And yet I think that I, who had vanished from his eyes,
Was still within him. For he, who painted me
In many scarlet dyes, came ere the end
To breathe forgiveness. I had once imagined
For his delight myself to be a maid
Bred on a fairy isle who knew not man,
And I played for him with what innocence
The maid would greet a lover who came to her.
And at the last he had fondled in his thought
My tender fantasy, and made himself
An enchanter with spirits at his command
And they had loved each other. So I think
That he had come to know himself and me.
O, why are we not certain of our fate!
There was another dread enchanter imagined.
A circle in the kingdom of the dead,
Where sinful lovers, who are blown about

In an eternal storm, cling to each other.
I thought that I, even on that stormy air,
Would have eternal joy were I the one
To whom his hands clung in the eternal shade.
And brooding on that poet's tale I dreamt
That I was so blown about with one
Who held to me, but when I saw his face
It was not the face I loved, but was the face
Beautiful, mad, hopeless, of that boy.
And I awoke. I had been weeping in sleep
And all my pillow was a wetness of tears.

EARTH SPIRIT

O dark holy magic,
To steal out at dawn,
To dip face and feet in grasses
The dew trembles on,
Ere its might of spirit healing
Be broken by the dawn.

O to reel drunken
On the heady dew,
To know again the virgin wonder
That boyhood knew,
While words run to music, giving voices
To the voiceless dew.

They will make, those dawn-wandering
Lights and airs,
The bowed worshipping spirit
To shine like theirs,
They will give to thy lips an aeolian
Music like theirs.

THE IRON AGE DEPARTS

They touched each other with wondering hands. No sultry fire
Stained the sweet crystal of spirit. They looked in each other's
    eyes
But saw there only the innocence of the wise,
No hiding beast. Had it flown, the dragon of desire?
Oh, what heroes, what strong immortal, overcame
That ancient evil? Again they were virginal,
Light and air made music as before the Fall.
Feet danced, hearts were airy, thoughts gay—gay as flame.
They ran to each other: "Are they indeed over, the long,
Unlit, black ages, crucifixions, agonies?"
They forgave unforgivable sins. All these
Old hates changed laughing into loves. All ancient wrong
Was heavenly Justice. They were drawn Into a fold
Where all things were in league. Even the stars drew nigh.
A marvelous sweetness breathed. Was it from earth or sky?
How came the heart to be melted? Was it the Age of Gold,
Fabulous, unhoped for, the sabbatical aeon of time,
Returned, not to rest in. No, but to hasten away,
For deeps within them called, divine dark deeps, where they
Beheld the fathers of being beckoning them to climb
To sit on thrones starry with the Ancestral Lights.
The wars of time were ended, the gates of the heart un barred.
A vastness flooded their being, a vastness myriad-starred.
The soul remembered its youth. Oh, in what deeps, what heights!
Then time turned on itself, yet the vision seemed so true
The heart ached to be prophet, to run through the streets and cry
"It is coming!—O, it Is coming! The Golden Age is nigh!
See what star-glimmering citadels rise in the blue!
What faces ancient with youth and wisdom watch from the
    towers,
For us who strayed, who were lost, who rise again from the dead.
For us, prodigals, the tables of heaven are spread;
From earth to heaven of heavens. All that glory is ours!"
And then the dragon croak of the city smote on my ears,
Harsh with the screech of wheels, the rasp of brakes. And I
Was again in the iron time. An unassailable sky.
Above, and darkness before us for blind uncountable years.

KARMA

All that was harsh or sweet
To me was brought
Through some affinity
With soul or sense or thought.
I complain not nor wonder.
Just was my lot.

I ask the wise to say
Why are we heir
To the wonder of the sky,
The shining there.
What justice gave to me
This star-enchanted air?

Is there still in us
A heaven-descended ray
Of that which built the palaces
Of night and day?
Do our first works, sun, moon, and stars,
Shine on our clay?

O, how my heart leaps up!
It can laugh. It could fly,
Even in dream being knit
To that majesty!
Though long passed from our glory,
I can sing! I could fly!

AN IDLE REVERIE

She passed by, shadowing the shining waters,
Noble and naiad-like her image, purpled
Against the sunblaze. As she wandered on
The old heart-sickness for beauty came upon me,
Because that imagination of her I had
Might shine on heaven or earth, be interlinked
With those pure, grave-eyed, immortal dawn-maidens
And glow unfading by them. It might be
The light of some long night in time; that beauty
Bowed to such sorrow that the soul beholding
From its transfiguring anguish must be born
Pure flame, as if it had known for itself
Of cross, of passion and the martyr's pyre.
And as from flowers that are invisible
Fragrance is blown, so from the vanished image
Fancies came thick, heart-troubling, honey-rich.
And I had woven my own enchantment then
And become slave to it. But remembrance came.
There had been nothing seen, nothing at all
But a radiant shadow in a blur of light.
Was it all self-begotten fantasy?
O agony of uncomprehended being
That I might never know why those divine
Dawn-maidens with so pure a lustre dwelt
For an Instant within me. Or why I dreamed
A martyrdom of innocent heroic youth;
Why an heart-aching love. O did her spirit
Carry in secret all its history,
Its starry dynasties from heaven to earth?
Was it whispered into my spirit in passing?
Did I imagine all from my own depths?
Is there a summit of being where the spirit,
An undraped fire, flashes its fire within
All other spirits, withholding nothing? Are
Our secret exaltations, ecstasies,
The loves more intimate than earth has given,
The martyrdoms as dark as Calvary,
Are they all born in that intensity
Of innumerable, interlinked being?
Is it because there nothing is withheld

And we are made richer by dream than life,
Our deepest love is given unto beauty
We have never seen, to lips we have never
Kissed nor heard in confession of love?
O might it be that in those reveries,
The moralist calls idle, there is wisdom
More precious than their virtue distils for us!
Our imaginations may be but flakes of fire
That drift upon us from the burning clouds
About a being that knows the innermost beat
Of every heart. Was it from that exhaustless
Secret well the soul of Shakespeare drew
To give us creatures that are not of himself?
O could our idleness grow to such virtue!
Our lonely reverie break into multitude!
How unwavering the will, how stern the heart,
To receive unbroken all that revelation,
The being of many risen within our own!
I tremble, fearful at the first glowing of
The magic-lovely, dragon-haunted air,
Where all beauty is shadowed by its demon,
And we are at once blessed and betrayed.
O child, who set my thoughts flying so far,
The ripples from thy passing feet have spread,
Not dying away, but gathering power to cast
Me heavenward, dizzy on their foam of light,
To beat at blazing gates, to cry on the Innermost
To know why I am so shaken by a shadow:
Not even a face seen, no heart-troubling eyes,
Only some wonder I imagined dwelling
In a radiant shadow in a blur of light.

FIRST LOVE

What treasure would we not have poured
At the white feet, when love had power,
If beauty that we had adored
Were tender to us for an hour.
I pass these burning memories. I
Run on to find a child who lay
On the warm earth, made tender by
A love breathed up from the dark clay.

How can I win that love again?
All I could bring to earth it owns,
What sacrifice must be, what pain
To be in league with these gray stones!

INCARNATION

Thou slender of limb; thou lightness;
Wild grace that flies
Over the shining sand
Under cloud-brilliant skies:
What beauty flies within thee,
Sped from what skies?

Thee for an instant
The god possesses,
Is joy in thy fleet limbs
Gay feet and flying tresses.
His lovely thought of thee the artist
Delights in and caresses.

Thou shalt remember hereafter
Through sorrowful years
That wonder of all thy moments,
And pine for through tears.
This moment that shall be for thee
A fountain of tears.

INNOCENCE

How could she know, that child who thought
So lovely pure the tale I told,
Within what obscene pits were wrought
The ores to make her fairy gold?

How could she know through what dire strife,
From what dark martyrdoms, there spring
The resurrection and the life,
The glow within the psyche's wing?

CABARET

The wave of life breaks there in froth,
A golden turbulence; and there
Proud boys, their thoughts gilded and gay,
Dance with their women light as air.

What Thought digs wide the pit of space?
What Will keeps the fierce stars apart?
What Titans build the dancing floor
For this soft indolence of heart?

While magic trifles, lips and eyes,
Catch at me through the wandering glow,
My heart feels moving in its deeps
The Great Deep's tidal under-tow.

MUSEUM

Why Sit I here communing
With shapes of the dead mind,
The outworn perfect beauty
The gods we left behind?

Though here all gods are gathered
The wonder has not grown.
The gods speak to us only
From their own natural throne.

Not here, but in wild places
Where wind and water reel
In ecstasy, light-stricken.
The gods may there reveal

The forms that hold the sceptre,
Brows bright with more than gold;
All that through lips of wonder
The sibyls breathed of old.

FOUNTAINS

That wild rose blossom
In sunlight or moonlight,
A fountain of its own beauty,
From hollow to height
Casts up its winged airy petals -
Transfigured light.

It shapes its delicate images
In light that all may see,
East, west, on height, in hollow,
Wherever eyes may be,
The vain lovely prodigal
Will give itself to thee.

O'er every bloom a nimbus
Of its own beauty rayed.
None by another's glory
Was cast into the shade.
It seemed the hollow of heaven
For each alone was made.

Wonder! wonder! wonder!
I saw in vision there
Myriads of fairy fountains
That cast upon the air
Their foam of phantom blossoms,
Upon the mystic air.

What could that light so laden
Be but the thought of One
That to the heaven of heavens
Can in an instant run,
Bearing that myriad beauty
Wider than moon or sun!

THE RIVER

There below me on the hillside where the glaring lantern burned
O what gay good-nights were shouted as the children homeward
    turned,
Running on the mountain ridges where the dizzy lantern made
Monstrous moths upon the midnight, flaring wings of light and
    shade.
Soon the merry voices faintly died upon the distant ridge,
And the giant moth had dwindled to the flicker of a midge,
And its light was lost amid the village lights of earth and sky.
Then a vast and silent river seemed to roll and pass me by.
On its tide the gay fleet-footed boys and girls were borne afar
To the port where sweep the golden galleons of sun and star,
With their merchandise of monarchs, glittering legions, tumult,
    flame,
And the heaven-assailing spirit and the clod without a fame,
In the anchorage of silence drop and vanish. As I lay
All but the desireless spirit seemed to roll and pass away.
And that spirit whispered to me: Time is but desire: its waves
Hurry onward on their flowing only those who are its slaves.
As I lay upon the hillside, I, whom love had lost and fled,
Knew I could be lost for ever and was strangely comforted.
Then that high desireless spirit in the stillness came more nigh,
Breathed within me for an instant, for an instant it was I.
For an instant I was nameless and unto myself unknown,
Nor knew I what looked on creation from that mountain seat alone.

EROS

How grave this night are earth and air!
The darkness hides under its fleece
The sombre stones 'mid which I lie
In their profundity of peace.

Above my savage couch I see,
Dark glowing through what endless heights,
The secret majesties of space,
Its still innumerable lights!

More ancient than all human love,
There lies between these things and me
Love, that through many a birth and death,
Shall grow as vast as that wide sea.

TWO VOICES

Body Speaks

The world wanders away from me.
Beauty and love are clouds gone by.
Heart is bereft of melody.
This that is left: O, is it I?

Why should a gorgeous cloth be spun
Bedecked with gem-like eye and wing,
Emblems of soul, as robe for one
That is, disrobed, so pale a thing?

Now all the colored winds are gone
Heart has not strength even to mourn.
All's numb but eyes that stare upon
The dust to which they shall return.

Soul Wakes

So, when sweet temple voices tire,
Will some one of a baser throng
From sleepy fingers steal the lyre
And drone to it so vile a song.

WHAT HOME

O, How I wreaked my childhood's spite
When I first dwindled to this day,
Thinking on my lost wonder world
That was so very far away.

And now my heart has come to rest,
Or the green earth has homelier grown.
Its children creep into my heart,
Woodland and water, hill and stone.

When I return to walk amid
The thrones of light, O shall I dream
Of the lost earth, a cloudy hill,
A shadowy vale, a flickering stream!

UNDERTONES

Beneath those sweet contented voices
A lovelier discontent,
All unknown to the gay singers
From hidden voices went.

Hardly a breath, almost inaudible,
A tone from distant spheres,
That wrought within me that enchantment
And stayed my listening ears.

Was it the buried spirit in them beating
Its love-fettered wings,
Prisoner within the heart and weeping
For what immortal things?

GROWTH

It is half an indignity and half a deliht
To know in age that I am but a child
Kept in a nursery. And yet we must
Be children of a king, pardoned so oft
Our passion fits, immodesties and noise,
Washed clean and dressed in shining raiment.
Here In this wide palace of air my spirit glows
With the gold and silver that it looks upon
As if it had never paddled in the mire.
Some majesty it must be ordered this
Transfiguration, the drapery of light
That I might come fitly unto the feast.
And this deep music of being in me, how
Could it be played upon my jangled strings
But by a master to whom the broken heart,
The listless will, the self-despisings, are
But notes that in the spirit melody
Had lost their sister notes, and sounding these
All breathe together in one melting chord.
O, what profundity, what gentleness
In power, to take what's base or fearful and
To find its place in beauty. I begin
To guess the infinite wisdom of the king,
And to what stature we must grow to come
To our inheritance, how airy delicate
The fingers holding the sceptre, and how deep
Must be the vision in brows that wear the crown.
For with what calm the princes of the stars
Carry the madness of battle on their orbs,
And yet the multitudinous agony
Must be theirs also. Are not the hands that strike
The stricken heart, within their sovereignty?
I sigh to think of all the toll to be
Ere we, who cry out at a prick of the thumb,
Can in the inexorable cavalcade
Ride on the power. And yet there is a joy
In contemplating the heroic gods,
The labor of the high, unshakeable ones
In whom the king has trust. For have we not
An infant spark of that which in the gods

Can pierce both heaven and brothel with its light
And be seduced neither by love nor hate,
But with the secret wisdom of their king
Weaving the richness of the universe
Into the least of things. So in our dark
Are breathings from the stars: no car but there
The majesty whispers itself: there's no exalted
Thought but the king gave unto it its light.
Dazed by excess of riches we do not know
That we are heaped with gifts from all the gods,
Microcosmos unconscious of itself.
And with this wisdom childhood ends, and all
Its songs are sung. I know a door has closed
Behind me and I can never again with joy
Live in that house. The arts that once were sweet
Would now be bitter in using. For not death
Which brings us back to life can take away
Age from the spirit. When again I try
To learn the starry alphabet of life
All I have passed through will be emptiness,
And only that have power which draws me to
The circle of wisdom. O, that I might be
A nameless vagrant without home, who yet
Could cry to the winds "Brother" as they pass,
And nod back at the stars, and so adore
The visible beauty that I may pass into
All that I contemplate, and feel the trees
Growing within me, men live, winds blow, seas roll
In the inner glory. Being so myriad I
Might forget I had a self and let the fullness
Be counselor unto me, and move as those
Born of the spirit, its messengers, whose ways
Are undecipherable as the winds,
And come at last after long tutelage
Nigh to the circle of wisdom, to those who shine
In ageless beauty and with smokeless light.

TO ONE WHO WANTED
A PHILOSOPHY FROM ME

You tell me of my songs you cannot fit
Their thought together, so contrary the lights.
 I cannot help you to the sense of it.
We rise and fall, have many days and nights,
Make songs in both; and when we are in our pit
Gaze back in wonder at our own endless heights.

THE SPELL

Now as I lean to whisper
To earth the last farewells,
The sly witch lays upon me
The subtlest of her spells:

Beauty that was not for me,
The love that was denied,
Their high disdainful sweetness
Now melted from their pride:

They run to me in vision,
All promise in their gaze,
All earth's heart-choking magic,
Madness of nights and days.

"These gifts are in my treasure,
Though fleeting be the breath;
Here only to wild giving
Is love made fire by death.

"This spell I put upon thee
Must, in thy being burn,
Till from the Heavenly City
To me thou shalt return."

A FAREWELL

I look on wood and hill and sky,
   Yet without any tears
To the warm earth I bid good-bye
   For what unnumbered years.

So many times my spirit went
   This dark transfiguring way,
Nor ever knew what dying meant,
   Deep night or a new day.

So many times it went and came,
   Deeper than thought it knows
Unto what majesty of flame
   In what wide heaven it goes.